WATERFALL WATCHERS

Pam Rosenberg

Raintree

Chicago, Illinois

www.heinemannraintree.com
Visit our website to find out
more information about
Heinemann-Raintree books.

To order:
☎ Phone 888-454-2279
🖥 Visit www.heinemannraintree.com
   to browse our catalog and order online.

Edited by Rebecca Rissman, Dan Nunn,
    and Sian Smith
Designed by Joanna Hinton Malivoire
Picture research by Elizabeth Alexander
Production by Victoria Fitzgerald
Originated by Capstone Global Library
Printed and bound in China by CTPS

15 14 13 12 11
10 9 8 7 6 5 4 3 2 1

**Library of Congress Cataloging-in-Publication
Data**
Rosenberg, Pam.
  Waterfall watchers / Pam Rosenberg.
    p. cm.—(Landform adventurers)
  Includes bibliographical references and index.
  ISBN 978-1-4109-4142-8 (hb)—ISBN 978-1-4109-4149-
7 (pb) 1. Waterfalls—Juvenile literature. I. Title.
  GB1403.8.R67 2012
  551.48'4—dc22   2010050067

Acknowledgments
We would like to thank the following for permission to
reproduce photographs: Alamy pp. 11 (© Paul Glendell),
14 (© Bert de Ruiter), 15 (© Greenshoots
Communications), 18 (© Alaska Stock LLC), 27 (© All
Canada Photos); Corbis pp. 8 (© Mike Grandmaison), 9
(© Jon Arnold/JAI), 23 (© Atlantide Phototravel); Getty
Images pp. 4 (Don Wilkie/Photodisc), 10 (Dave & Les
Jacobs/Blend Images), 13 (Alan Smith/Stone); Photolibrary
pp. 12 (Keith Douglas), 21 (Yoshio Tomii Photo Studio),
24 (Gavin Hellier), 26 (Darwin Wiggett), 28 (JTB Photo),
29 (Alaska Stock Images); Rex Features p. 20 (© W.
Disney/Everett); Science Photo Library pp. 7 (Gary
Hincks), 16 (Pascal Goetgheluck), 17 (Pascal
Goetgheluck); Shutterstock pp. 5 (© Hugo Maes), 6 (©
Kevin Tavares), 19 (© oksana.perkins), 22 (© InnaFelker).

Cover photograph of a man climbing down a waterfall
reproduced with permission of Alamy (© blickwinkel).

Every effort has been made to contact copyright holders
of material reproduced in this book. Any omissions will
be rectified in subsequent printings if notice is given to
the publisher.

Some words are shown in bold, **like this**. You can find
out what they mean by looking in the glossary.

Contents

Thundering Water

Imagine that you are walking along a fast-moving river. You hear a sound like thunder. It's getting louder and louder. The river suddenly drops hundreds of feet! The water crashes down, sending up a spray. It's a waterfall!

spray

Maria Cristina Falls, Philippines

What Is a Waterfall?

Waterfalls are places where **riverbeds** suddenly drop. Big drops can form when part of the riverbed is made of soft rock. The soft rock wears away more quickly than hard rock and leaves a drop.

Waterfalls can also form in spots where Earth's **crust** moves. Sometimes one piece ends up higher than the other. Then, river water falls over the edge of the higher piece.

crust

Some waterfalls are known as **cascade** waterfalls. They are usually smaller drops. Often, the water falls over a group of rocks that look like stairs.

cascade waterfall

cataract waterfall

Cataract waterfalls are big, powerful waterfalls. A lot of water plunges over a steep cliff.

Waterfall Scientists

Waterfalls are beautiful. Some people like them so much that they decide to make waterfall watching their jobs!

- **Geologists** study rocks that make up the **riverbed**.
- **Hydrologists** study how water flows and changes the landscape.
- **Ecologists** study how waterfalls affect nearby plants and animals.

This ecologist is examining moss growing near a waterfall.

Moving Back

Did you know that a waterfall moves back over time? It happens because the rushing water wears away the rocks it flows over. This is called **erosion**.

Some geologists study rocks to find out how quickly a waterfall is moving back or how it formed.

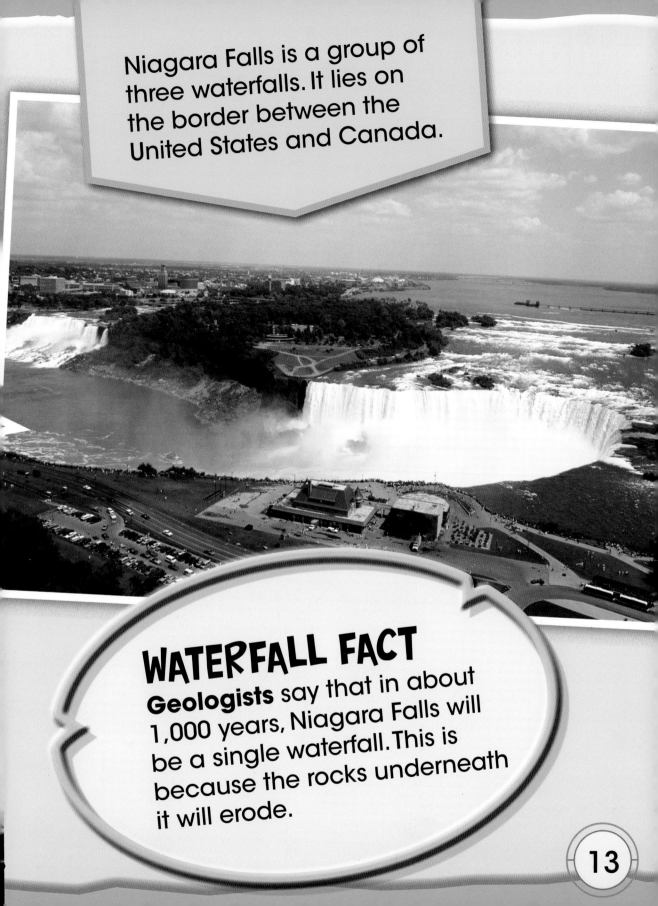

Niagara Falls is a group of three waterfalls. It lies on the border between the United States and Canada.

WATERFALL FACT

Geologists say that in about 1,000 years, Niagara Falls will be a single waterfall. This is because the rocks underneath it will erode.

Waterfall-Watcher Tools

Geologists use tools to learn about waterfalls. They use rock hammers to help them take samples of rocks. Special **compasses** and **GPS receivers** help them to map the rocks of the waterfall.

People use GPS to find out where places are.

rock hammer

Hydrologists are interested in finding out more about how a river's water flows. They may fill containers with water to see how clean it is. Or they might use a special pole to see how deep the water is or how quickly it is moving.

container

Collecting water from waterfalls can sometimes be dangerous. Scientists need to wear special safety gear.

Many plants and animals live near rivers. **Ecologists** study how the moving water affects living things. They use tools such as nets to capture animals. Sometimes they take animals away in tanks so they can study them.

salmon

WATERFALL FACT
Salmon swim upstream and even leap up waterfalls. Why? They go back to where they were born to lay their eggs.

Extreme Waterfalls

The tallest waterfall in the world is in Venezuela. The local people call it Kerepakupai Merú, which means "waterfall of the deepest place." It is known by many people as Angel Falls.

Angel Falls was the model for the waterfall in the movie *Up*.

Angel Falls, Venezuela

WATERFALL FACT
Angel Falls is 3,212 feet tall. That is taller than two Willis Towers stacked on top of each other!

Victoria Falls is sometimes called the world's largest curtain of water. It lies between the countries of Zimbabwe and Zambia. The people who live near the falls call it Mosi-oa-Tunya, which means "The Smoke That Thunders."

Spray from the Victoria Falls looks a bit like smoke.

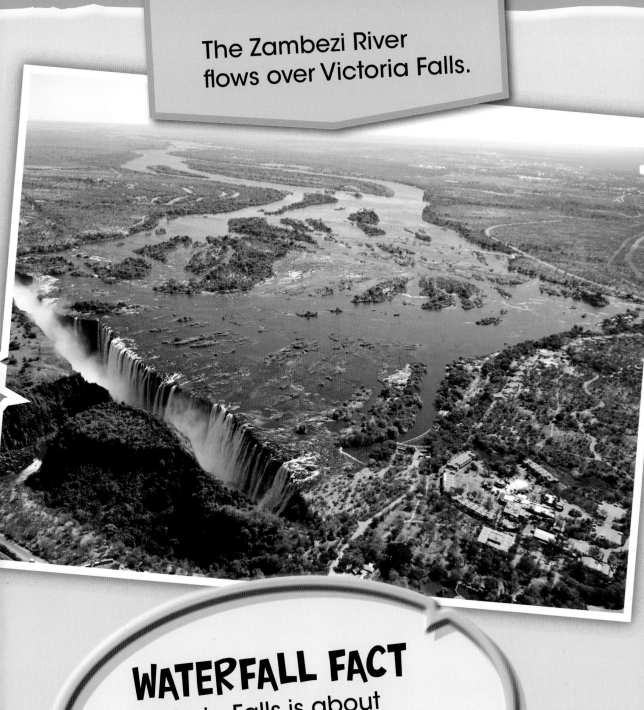

The Zambezi River flows over Victoria Falls.

WATERFALL FACT
Victoria Falls is about 5,600 feet wide! That is almost the length of 19 football fields!

Waterfalls of the World

There are many amazing waterfalls around the world. Some are even found underground!

WATERFALL FACT

Ruby Falls, in Tennessee, is 1,120 feet below the surface of a mountain. That is just a bit shorter than the Empire State Building!

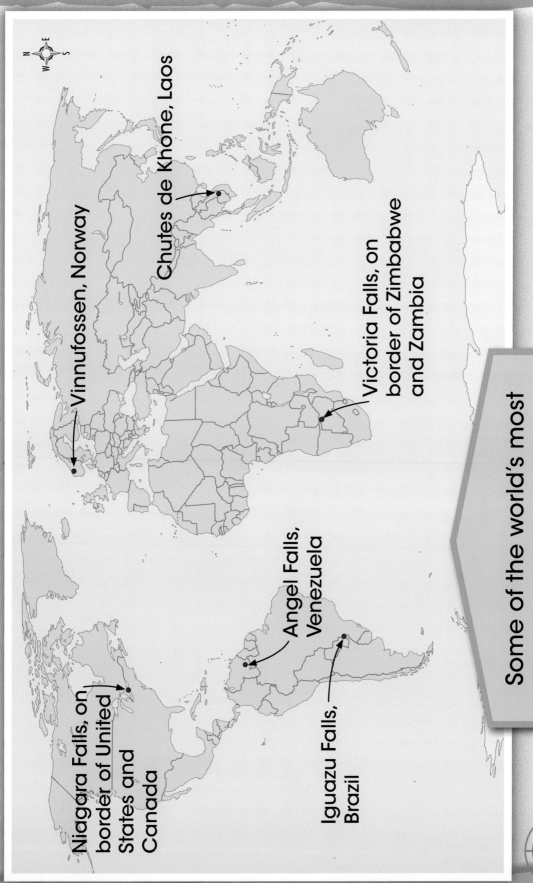

Vinnufossen, Norway

Chutes de Khone, Laos

Victoria Falls, on border of Zimbabwe and Zambia

Niagara Falls, on border of United States and Canada

Angel Falls, Venezuela

Iguazu Falls, Brazil

Some of the world's most famous waterfalls are shown on this map.

Not Just a Pretty Rock Face

Waterfall scientists know there is a lot more to waterfalls than just how beautiful they are. **Hydroelectric** power plants can be built at waterfalls. They use the energy of the moving water to provide electricity for millions of people.

This hydroelectric power plant is at Niagara Falls, in New York.

Becoming a Waterfall Watcher

Do you want to be a waterfall watcher? Learn more about waterfalls around the world. Study science and math in school. Plan a trip to go and see a waterfall.

You often need to go hiking or use a canoe to get to waterfalls, so stay strong and fit. Who knows? Maybe one day you will discover something new about waterfalls!

Glossary

cascade type of waterfall, especially one made up of a series of steps

cataract large waterfall, especially one that flows over a steep cliff

compass tool used for finding directions

crust hard outer layer of Earth

ecologist scientist who studies living things and the places where they live

erosion wearing away of rock by the action of water, wind, or ice

geologist scientist who studies Earth's layers of soil and rock

GPS receiver tool that helps people determine their location by receiving signals from satellites that orbit Earth

hydroelectric electricity produced by moving water

hydrologist scientist who studies water

riverbed channel that contains rivers

Find Out More

Find out

Can a waterfall freeze?

Books

Claybourne, Anna. *100 Things You Should Know About Extreme Earth.* Broomall, Pa.: Mason Crest, 2009.

Schuh, Mari. *Natural Wonders: Waterfalls.* Mankato,Minn.: Capstone, 2011.

Tieck, Sarah. *All Aboard America: Niagara Falls.* Edina, Minn.: ABDO, 2008.

Websites

http://kids.nationalgeographic.com/kids/ games/puzzlesquizzes/waterfalls-puzzler/ Try completing waterfall jigsaw puzzles on this website.

http://science.howstuffworks.com/waterfall- pictures.htm Visit this website to see pictures of several different waterfalls.

Index